Original title:
Petals on the Page

Copyright © 2025 Creative Arts Management OÜ
All rights reserved.

Author: Helena Marchant
ISBN HARDBACK: 978-1-80566-627-1
ISBN PAPERBACK: 978-1-80566-912-8

The Aroma of Written Spring

In the garden of ink, a story blooms,
With laughter and whimsy, it brightly looms.
Each word like a flower, colors set free,
Tickling the senses as silly as can be.

The nouns dance around like bees with delight,
Chasing verbs that buzz from morning till night.
Adjectives giggle, they prance and they sway,
While adverbs spin circles, yelling, "Hooray!"

A comma trips over, falls flat on its face,
Creating a pause in this riotous race.
It laughs, gets back up, says, "What was I here?"
A brief moment stalls in the fresh spring air.

Each line is a petal, a burst of good cheer,
Scattering laughter, drawing us near.
In the bloom of the text, we find joy's embrace,
As the aroma of spring makes a merry place.

Letters from a Blossoming Soul

In the garden, I found a quill,
Written by a daffodil!
It scribbled thoughts so bright and bold,
Of secrets waiting to be told.

It wished to dance in morning light,
With petals shimmying in delight.
While bees buzzed tunes like happy fools,
And laughed at all the paper rules.

Oh, the stories flowers share,
Of bees that prance without a care.
They giggle as the sunbeams play,
In their own silly, floral way.

So take a pen, let colors blend,
And hear the laughter flowers send.
For words can bloom in every mind,
Just like the petals left behind!

Ink Drops and Floral Hues

A drop of ink fell from the sky,
And landed where the daisies lie.
They giggled with a cheeky grin,
As wild ideas began to spin.

With colors bold, they made a mess,
Creating art in soft excess.
Tulips turned into typing trees,
Chuckling at the light spring breeze.

A rose wrote sonnets, oh so sweet,
With prickly thoughts, it skipped a beat.
While violets painted jokes anew,
Scribbled with laughter, bright, and true.

So let your thoughts blossom and bloom,
In every spot, there's ample room.
With ink and flair, let humor fly,
For flowers know, the time is nigh!

Threads of Nature Woven in Words

In a tapestry of bright delight,
Nature's threads weave day and night.
A sunflower stitched a tale with glee,
Of how to brew sweet honey tea.

Lilies laughed at rhymes so bold,
While violets whispered tales of old.
They threaded jokes through every seam,
Like petals sprouting from a dream.

With every stitch, a giggle sang,
As tulips joined the joyful clang.
They danced around with every rhyme,
Creating laughter, one step at a time.

So grab your needles, join the fun,
Woven stories are never done.
In nature's quilt, we find our place,
Where humor blooms with every trace!

Blossoms of Imagination's Quill

A quill once danced on petals bright,
Sketching visions in the light.
It penned a tale of silly sights,
With blooms that wore their finest tights.

A marigold proclaimed with cheer,
"There's laughter in the atmosphere!"
It twirled around with vibrant flair,
As dandelions ruffled their hair.

With every stroke, the colors flashed,
As daisies giggled, unabashed.
The paper turned to gardens wide,
Where imagination loved to glide.

So take your quill and join the spree,
In this grand garden jubilee.
For every word's a flower's bloom,
Creating joy that fills the room!

From Ink to Bloom: A Journey

Inkwells spill tales of whimsy,
Words dance like bees on sunny scenes.
Marks upon the parchment sway,
Chasing paper dreams all day.

Quills take flight in hopeful glee,
As laughter drips from each decree.
Writers giggle, twist, and twine,
Crafting blooms in every line.

Each joke soars like a bright balloon,
Bouncing lightly to a sunny tune.
With every stroke, a chuckle grows,
Their silly schemes in ink compose.

A garden blooms with every pun,
Where laughter joins the inked-up fun.
Pages flutter, petals flare,
In the joyous chaos, who wouldn't care?

The Floral Legacy of Inked Words

Inkweed fields stretch wide and far,
Stories sprout like tiny stars.
Each line a petal, fresh and bright,
Whispering secrets day and night.

A daisy chain of witty quips,
Sprouting from the writer's tips.
Gardens grow from scribbled dreams,
Where laughter flows in vibrant streams.

In this plot of jumbled lines,
Silly thoughts form quirky vines.
Each phrase a bud, each laugh a cheer,
Cultivating joy while we appear.

So let your ink take flight and share,
With sunny words filling the air.
A legacy of giggles sown,
In every story, a seed is grown.

Poetry in the Garden's Embrace

In gardens where the daisies sprout,
Poets roam with joyful shout.
Mirthful verses spritz like dew,
In every rhyme, a chuckle or two.

Worms in hats, earthworms in suit,
Composing sonnets to the root.
Petunias giggle, the roses tease,
As ink drips down in silly ease.

Mushrooms play the ukulele strum,
While bees buzz softly, having fun.
Each stanza leaps like frogs in spring,
In this garden, laughter is king.

With every garden's silly scheme,
Words blossom like a vibrant dream.
In grey ink's whirl, the joy we trace,
Creating poetry in nature's grace.

Brushstrokes of Nature's Whispers

Whimsical brushstrokes paint the sky,
Nature giggles as butterflies fly.
Every stroke a burst of grins,
Where silliness twirls and begins.

Colorful words tumble from the tree,
Just like fruits, so sweet and free.
Sunlit laughter spills from ink,
A funny twist, a playful wink.

In this garden, every leaf knows,
The secrets of laughter that grows.
Stories sway with the breezy vibes,
As flowers lip-sync to joyful jibes.

So take your brush and spin it fast,
Let giggles bloom, let worries pass.
For in this world of wild delight,
Nature whispers jokes, oh so light.

Fragments of Nature's Scribbles

A bee flew in, oh what a sight,
Was trying to dance with a flower so bright.
The daisy just waved, gave a little cheer,
While the tulip laughed, 'Get out of here!'

Leaves were giggling, tickled by the breeze,
Trees shared gossip like old friends at ease.
A squirrel took notes in the bark's secret text,
Declared it a meeting, nature perplexed!

The wind brought whispers, secrets untold,
Of blooms that socked it, humor bold.
Nature's ink spills where laughter cascades,
Crafting the quirkiest of leafy charades.

In this garden, where silliness reigns,
Each verse a chuckle across the lanes.
A scribe of pollen, with laughter, we scribble,
In fragments of nature, the glee is a dribble.

Inked Garden Serenade

The roses grumbled, 'We're too fancy!'
While daisies play footsie – how chancy!
The violets chuckled at a bumblebee,
Who fumbled and tumbled, not quite so free.

A snail recited a love-struck tune,
A lilac blushed beneath the full moon.
The daisies all giggled, 'Just pick a flower!'
And the sunflowers rolled, hour by hour.

A butterfly flitted, a dance in air,
While petals debated if they'd dare.
They wrote a script that nature could star,
Of snickers and spills, a bright garden bazaar.

So let the petals sing their sweet refrain,
Of joyful shenanigans, like a wild train.
In this garden, laughter is the art,
Where ink from the flowers flows straight from the heart.

A Canvas of Petal-Laced Thoughts

The tulips told tales that stretched so long,
Of deer who pranced and sang silly songs.
The lilacs chimed in, with wit and cheer,
While the daisies danced, defying all fear.

A funny bee wore a tiny bow tie,
Buzzed by the hostas, oh me, oh my!
The sunflowers wore hats, oh so absurd,
While daisies rolled laughter, quite unheard.

The garden held secrets, jokes on display,
Where crickets cracked puns and butterflies play.
A canvas of bloom, in colors so bright,
Each bloom painted smiles, what a sweet sight!

So sprinkle your laughter as petals take flight,
In a garden where joy dances day and night.
With whimsy and mirth, nature's delight,
A tapestry woven with sheer delight.

Scrolls of Wilderness Dreams

A feathered friend perched high on a branch,
Proposed a grand game of 'dare to inch a chance'.
The dandelions puffed out in delight,
While zany old weeds wrangled through the night.

In the meadow, a frog donned a top hat,
Said he was off to a formal chit-chat.
The cattails giggled, all swaying along,
Jumping in sync, they joined in the song.

The brook babbled secrets, gossip to share,
While squirrels debated in flair and in pair.
It's a wild affair in the canvas we roam,
Each scroll of the realm feels just like home.

So capture the laughter in nature's own dreams,
For wilderness whispers of zany schemes.
With petals as pages, let the fun begin,
In this playful landscape, where smiles always win.

Rhythms of Nature's Palette

In gardens where the daisies dance,
The bees wear tiny pants.
A butterfly forgot its lunch,
And now the flowers look like they munch.

The sun's a chef with bright delight,
Cooking rays both warm and bright.
The wind plays tag with leafy hats,
While squirrels plot their acorn chats.

Grass tickles toes with playful glee,
As ants march by in a line so free.
A rainbow's laugh spills on the ground,
Nature's giggle is all around.

With every bloom, a silly joke,
As clouds above begin to poke.
And if you listen, nature sings,
Of biscuit trees and jellybean springs.

Stanzas in Full Bloom

Oh look, the roses wear a crown,
While tulips sport their bright nightgown.
The sunflowers nod with silly glee,
As if discussing some mystery.

The garden's a stage for critters' fun,
Where ladybugs play hopscotch in the sun.
A caterpillar shows off its tie,
Saying, "I'm not shy, I'm just spry!"

The daisies gossip, petals in whirl,
About the beetle that gave them a twirl.
Underneath, the worms throw a rave,
Mixing the dirt like nature's fave.

With laughter spilled upon the ground,
Every sprout shares giggles abound.
Watch closely now, the jesters bloom,
As nature writes its own cartoon.

Lines of a Garden Sonnet

In patches bright, the colors play,
Where flowers tease the sun all day.
The bees, they buzz like little cars,
And dress in stripes with flair from Mars.

A gopher winks, its burrow a maze,
While petals sway in merry craze.
The daffodils dance on the breeze,
While sunlight tickles the bumblebees.

Oh, check the thyme near the old oak tree,
It's having a party, just you and me!
With rosemary wearing a fancy hat,
And minty breath from an odd little cat.

Laughter echoes from the blooming crowd,
As plants perform, oh so very loud.
In this garden of whimsy and cheer,
Life scribbles joy that's perfectly clear.

The Symphony of Written Blossoms

With petals like notes in a joyful tune,
The flowers sway under the bright, full moon.
A melody strums through the breezy air,
As crickets tap-dance without a care.

The daffodils giggle, a sweet serenade,
While poppies in red wear a polka dot shade.
In every corner, nature's prance,
As veggies decide to start a dance.

Each leaf's a page in this wondrous book,
Where insects gather to take a look.
The worms compose a sonnet underground,
While frogs croak out a ribbit sound.

With laughter blooming by day and night,
Watch nature's folly and pure delight.
For every flower boasts its own flair,
Creating a symphony, oh so rare!

Nature's Chronicle of Silken Lines

In gardens where the daisies play,
The bunnies hop and dance all day.
They munch on carrots, so divine,
While squirrels debate the best way to dine.

The sun flips pancakes up in the sky,
And butterflies wear ties oh so spry.
The bees hold concerts, buzzing so keen,
While ants form bands in a grassy green.

With laughter carried on the breeze,
The flowers giggle with such ease.
Each bloom a jest, a secret shared,
In nature's book, we're all prepared.

So gather round, let's read aloud,
The tales of flora, funny and proud.
In every stem and leaf we find,
A quirky story intertwined.

The Canvas of Blossoms and Words

A painter's brush with colors bright,
Mixes giggles in the morning light.
The lilies laugh, the roses blush,
While daffodils perform a rush.

The canvas drips with honeyed cheer,
As gardeners cheer, 'Let's spread good cheer!'
With paintbrushes made of dandelion,
They create scenes that are sheer divine!

Gnomes in hats with wobbly feet,
Join forces with bees for a garden beat.
Each petal whispers a fun little rhyme,
Making nature's art stand the test of time.

The colors groove, they twirl and swirl,
Bringing smiles to every young girl.
On this canvas, joy just won't cease,
Nature and laughter share a feast.

A Lyric in the Garden's Embrace

In the patio, laughter blooms,
With turtles trying on flower costumes.
Sunflowers dance in silly poses,
While tangled vines wear playful noses.

The crickets chirp a jazzy beat,
As ladybugs tap their tiny feet.
The daisies twirl in their bright attire,
Conducting wind like a true choir.

A cheeky gopher pokes out his head,
To steal the shine from the roses' spread.
"Hey!" shouts a fern, "Get back in your hole!
You've turned my day into a stroll!"

So here we gather, smiles all around,
With silly stories nature has found.
In laughs and lyrics, we all participate,
In the garden, laughter's the perfect fate.

Poetry Wrapped in Floral Elegance

A corsage of laughter, oh what a sight,
As petals spin dreams in the soft moonlight.
The violets whisper in tones of mirth,
As tulips twirl, celebrating their birth.

With hummingbirds dressed in snazzy suits,
They dance around in their fancy boots.
Petunias gossip in colors bright,
Sharing secrets that feel just right.

Sunshine and shadows play a game,
Planting giggles in nature's name.
Each bloom a verse, a pun to ignite,
The hilarity of the stars at night.

With poetry stitched in floral lace,
Nature smiles with an inviting grace.
We prance through verses, side by side,
In this garden, where joy and fun abide.

Lines from the Heart of Spring

In the garden, jokes take flight,
Flowers giggle, oh what a sight.
Bees buzz in a comic buzz,
Nature's punchlines, just because.

The sun wears shades, it's feeling cool,
Plants throw parties, who needs a pool?
Butterflies dance in silly rows,
While the tulips giggle, nobody knows.

Squirrels prank with acorn toss,
A leaf slips by in a leafy gloss.
Laughter sprouts in every nook,
Spring's a book, come take a look!

Beware of daisies with a flair,
Whispering secrets in the air.
Every bloom brings chuckles near,
In this season, joy is clear!

A Poetic Fragrance Laid Bare

Scented rhymes float, a silly tease,
Daffodils tickle in the breeze.
Jokes unfold in grassy plays,
While the sun dips in golden rays.

A rose winks with a cheeky grin,
Says to the tulip, 'Let's begin!'
"Knock, knock" giggles the garden gate,
"Who's there?" asks the strawberry plate.

Laughter bounces from leaf to leaf,
A petunia's pun brings comic relief.
In the hedges, whispers take flight,
Nature's jesters dance through the night.

With every color, a laugh erupts,
While the violets share their hiccups.
In this fragrant prankster's den,
Joy blooms anew, again and again!

The Blossoming Script

In the morning light, jokes unfold,
Writing stories, bold and gold.
A sunflower tips its hat with flair,
While daisies whisper a playful dare.

The ink of skies, so blue and bright,
Scribbles laughter through day and night.
A bumblebee hums a silly tune,
While petals dance 'neath the laughing moon.

Wispy clouds join in the fun,
Sketching shadows as they run.
The grass plots laughter on the plot,
Nature's humor - forget-me-not!

So let the blooms tell tales of glee,
In every corner, smiles run free.
With every line, spring scripts its play,
In a garden where jokes save the day!

Verses of Petal-Wrapped Memories

Bright memories swirl like fragrant air,
Petals whisper tales without a care.
A daisy sits with a twisty grin,
Sharing secrets that make you spin.

Tulips giggle with pom-pom hats,
As nearby bees engage in chats.
"Who was that?" asks a shy marigold,
"Weren't they here?"—that's spring, so bold!

In the breeze, laughter rustles leaves,
Comical tales that nature weaves.
A trailing vine slips with a wink,
"Did you hear?" and we all think.

With every bloom, a jest is told,
In the warm sun, all hearts unfold.
So gather 'round, let the chuckles fly,
In this garden where joys never die!

Whispers in a Floral Diary

In the garden, I found a bee,
Writing notes just for me.
It buzzed tales of nectar flows,
While dodging gnats in floral bows.

Roses giggled with a wink,
While daisies danced, I think.
Tulips donned their sassy hats,
As I scribbled down their chats.

A sunflower spilled its sunny jest,
Claiming it's the very best.
But when it saw the morning glories,
It faded fast, with silly stories.

So pass the pen, oh let it glide,
In nature's book, let joy abide.
Each line a cheer, each word a bloom,
In this floral fun, there's always room.

Pages Filled with Blooming Thoughts

In a notebook bound with vine,
Pansies plot how to dine.
They dream of cakes and fruity treats,
While giggling among their leafy seats.

Dandelions penned a crafty scheme,
To become the world's best ice cream.
With flavors wild and colors bright,
They'd start a scoop fight, oh what a sight!

Lilies whispered, 'Is it time?'
To dance beneath the sun's sweet rhyme?
With twirls and laughs, they all agreed,
To throw a bash, oh yes indeed!

And so the pages filled with cheer,
In this garden diary, all are near.
With every scratch, a joyful twist,
In blooming thoughts that can't be missed.

Verses Beneath the Cherry Blossoms

Under blooms of pink delight,
Silly squirrels took to flight.
They danced and twirled on branches high,
While rapping rhymes that made me sigh.

"Hey, humans, don't you see?
These blossoms are just for me!"
The robins crooned a cheeky song,
As petals rained down all day long.

A chipmunk scribbled post-it notes,
To remind us of their wily oats.
"Do not disturb, we're on a spree,
With cherry snacks and herbal tea!"

So here I sit, beneath the trees,
Laughing at the buzzing bees.
Each verse they share, a silly dance,
In nature's script, I find my chance.

Inked Leaves and Floral Tales

In a meadow where colors clash,
Butterflies strut in a dazzling flash.
They wrote a story of their flights,
With crayons made of sunlight bites.

Poppy petals joined the fun,
Inking tales of a racing run.
They sported shades both bold and bright,
While sharing giggles, such pure delight.

The daisies fumbled with their pens,
Drawing circles, making friends.
"Oh, let's create a flower band!"
As bees would hum, and leaves would stand.

So grab a leaf, an inkling too,
Join the show, we'll welcome you!
In this floral tale, we burst and bloom,
With laughter echoing, sweet perfume.

Verses of a Sunlit Meadow

In a field of blooms, where laughter grows,
The daisies dance, in silly rows.
A bumblebee hums a tune so sweet,
While flirtatious flowers compete for heat.

With tulips dressed in polka dots,
They gossip secrets, connecting the knots.
A buttercup tries to show some class,
But blooms with style, and lets out gas.

Rhythms of Growth and Expression

Roots intertwine in quirky ways,
Whispering jokes on sunny days.
The fern declares, with utmost pride,
"I'm the fittest in leafy hide!"

A dandelion puffs with glee,
"Watch me fly, I'm a weed-to-be!"
While sunflowers rotate, a determined crew,
Mimicking ballerinas… oh the view!

The Symphony of Stems and Sentences

Beneath the sigh of a willow's sways,
A chorus of stems sings silly plays.
The roses laugh with their thorny jabs,
As violets wear their sassy rags.

A daffodil dreams of becoming a star,
But tripping on roots is just who you are.
With each little bloom, the giggles arise,
In the garden's absurd, where humor flies.

Words Adrift in Petal Rain

Speaking in colors, the blossoms chime,
Their rhymes are a jester's sunlit prime.
As petals fall like confetti blare,
They tickle the funny bones in the air.

Butterflies chuckle at silly sights,
As blossoms twirl in carefree flights.
With laughter sprouting from the ground,
Nature's hilarity knows no bound.

Pages Breathing with Aroma

Ink spills on the paper's face,
Dancing shadows take their place.
The whiff of words fills the air,
Like snacks left out, a funny share.

Each line a flower, freshly found,
Giggles echo, laughter bound.
The margins bloom with silly glee,
As pens spill chaos, wild and free.

Aha! That joke, oh what a pun,
Inky blooms, oh what fun!
A garden grows with every page,
A riot of wit, on the stage.

Who knew that prose could smell like tea?
These verses sprout, just wait and see!
With every turn, a fragrance bright,
A comedic waltz, pure delight.

The Scent of Written Beauty

Open up that book of cheer,
A whiff of laughter's drawing near.
With every word, a joke unspools,
Like wildflowers breaking rules.

Sticky notes, a colorful mess,
Oh look, another faux distress!
The chapters bloom in shades of jest,
When humor's on the writer's quest.

Ink-splash giggles, what a sight,
A garden of quips, pure delight.
The prose perfumes with silly might,
As rhymes take wing, a joyful flight!

Who knew that writing could smell so bright?
Each page a garden, playful and light.
Puns in petals, a fragrant delight,
Humor blooms in every bite.

Blooms in Every Written Breath

With every breath, a bloom takes flight,
The words giggle, oh what a sight!
They flutter like butterflies in play,
Creating chaos in a funny way.

A quick quip here and a pun there,
Scribbled flowers dance without care.
Every sentence, a petal's flight,
Tickling the air with pure delight.

In this wild garden of written jest,
Each line a laugh, oh what a fest!
With humor sprouting left and right,
Endless blooms in gleeful light.

So flip the pages, take a look,
At this garden spun from a book.
In every breath, a chuckle's breath,
A floral joke that laughs at death.

Chronicle of Blossoms in Verse

Scribbles rise like blooms in spring,
Each verse a joke, a humorous fling.
Life's a garden, oh so spry,
With laughter twirling in the sky.

The ink flows like a river fair,
Dancing flowers everywhere.
Oh look, a line with sprightly cheer,
It tickles the senses, make it clear.

The chronicles of humor swell,
In every letter, a joking spell.
Pages open, blossoms fly,
Their fragrance rich, oh me, oh my!

A garden grows in a book's embrace,
Words bloom bright in a funny race.
So come and see this written spree,
Where silliness thrives in harmony.

The Dance of Inkwell and Fern

Inkwell sways with a splash and a swirl,
Fern giggles, doing a twirl.
Scribbles tumble, words take flight,
As they dance in the soft moonlight.

Splatters of ink on an eager page,
Frolicking freely, the words engage.
A giggly garden of silly rhymes,
Chasing after jumbled times.

The quill quivers in delight,
Tickling ferns, oh what a sight!
Letters jiggle, hiccup, and hop,
In the merry inkwell, they never stop!

With a flourish, they leap with glee,
In a playful game of ink and spree.
Nature's laughter spills and flows,
As each silly stanza grows.

Nature's Palette upon the Scroll

A canvas spills with colors bright,
Nature grins, what a sight!
Crayons giggle, they get in line,
To color words in sunshine divine.

Green grass wiggles, a playful tease,
While blossoms chuckle in the breeze.
A stroke of red, a splatter of blue,
All join in, saying, "Wahoo!"

The scroll wiggles, it can't resist,
As colors dance, a twisty twist!
A harmony of hues leads the way,
Nature's laughter upon display.

Pencils hum a jolly tune,
Painting laughter, morning to moon.
Words take flight, as colors sway,
In this whimsical, artsy fray.

Stanzas of a Blooming Eden

In Eden's heart where blooms erupt,
Stanzas spring, all raucous and corrupt.
Petals prance in an eager line,
Roses chuckle, saying, "I'm divine!"

Daisies spar in a playful bout,
Joked with pollen, all about.
Verses bounce like bees on flowers,
Finding giggles in springtime hours.

Lilies laugh under the sun,
While clever violets have their fun.
They wave to words as they slip and slide,
In this Eden, a giddy ride.

With each new stanza, laughter blooms,
As words create a symphonic tune.
In this garden where humor thrives,
Poetic joy—Eden arrives!

Echoes of Green Beneath the Words

Beneath the scribbles, whispers play,
Echoes of green have their say.
Grass giggles as it tapes its tale,
While inklings swirl like a happy gale.

Lush ideas sprout with a pop,
Wiggly words that never flop.
Each letter jumps like a froggy quest,
And nature laughs, feeling quite blessed.

Tickled leaves take to the sky,
Punning trees that wave goodbye.
With every word, laughter spins,
As echoes of green invite grins.

So write your joy upon the page,
Let green giggles break the cage.
In the forest's embrace, let humor ring,
With echoes beneath, let the laughter sing!

Enchanted Scribbles of Spring's Glow

A doodle danced across the floor,
With colors bright, it begged for more.
The bees waged war on a cupcake sweet,
While squirrels juggled acorns at my feet.

The flowers giggled in the breeze,
Tickling bumblebees with ease.
A wobbly worm tried to take flight,
Wishing on stars while munching a bite.

Grasshoppers leaped with comic flair,
Playing hopscotch without a care.
I laughed so hard, I couldn't stand,
Nature's circus, perfectly planned!

So here we scribble, with colors bold,
In the book of spring, stories unfold.
Each mark a laugh, each line a cheer,
As nature's ink brings joys near.

The Romance of Nature and Ink

A pen fell in love with a charming flower,
Together they danced for an hour.
With every stroke, the petals swirled,
In this sweet union, laughter twirled.

The ink spilled secrets on the ground,
As chirping birds gathered around.
They started a band, with notes so light,
Singing to the moon all through the night.

An artist painted a rainbow sigh,
While cheese-loving bugs wiggled by.
With each brush, a story was spun,
In the garden of giggles, we all had fun.

So here we find, in nature's embrace,
The joy of words in this gleeful space.
With ink and blooms in a wild dance,
A romance written by chance!

Whispers of Fragrant Ink

In a meadow where daisies sway,
A wise old quill began to play.
Whispers flowed on a breeze so sweet,
Tickling the toes of butterflies' feet.

The ink pot bubbled with laughter loud,
As ants joined in, feeling so proud.
Dandelions giggled, wishing to fly,
While chubby snails gave it a try.

Oh, what fun, under sun-soaked skies,
As flowers and bugs conspire and rise.
Each line a chuckle, each dot a gleam,
In the story of nature, we dance and dream.

So let's dip our pens, and scribble away,
With giggles and joy, we will always stay.
In fragrant whispers, let's twirl and spin,
As ink and blossoms invite us in!

Pages Adrift in Bloom

Oh look, a notebook gone astray,
Drifting on leaves, come out to play!
A butterfly perched, reading in glee,
Scribbled tales beneath the tree.

The wind played tricks, flipping each sheet,
As ladybugs danced to a bug-eyed beat.
Petunia was writing about her grand day,
While the sunbeams sent cloud friends away.

With colored grass and a rainbow blend,
Each page a story, a giggle to send.
Crickets sang ballads of rhythmic fun,
In the giggle-fuelled pages, we all spun.

So grab your pen and join the spree,
In this book of wonders, wild and free.
Nature laughs as we scribble and zoom,
With pages adrift in joyful bloom!

The Tapestry of Nature's Script

In gardens bright, the flowers sigh,
They write their notes, oh me, oh my!
With bees as scribes, they buzz and hum,
Each petal's tale, a blooming drum.

A daisy winks, a rose does tease,
They giggle soft in the gentle breeze.
The sunbeams laugh, they dance around,
As nature's jokes are shared, unbound.

The wind becomes the mischief's muse,
It tickles leaves, gives nature a ruse.
The tulips nod, the violets snicker,
In this grand play, the laughter's quicker.

Oh, what a script this garden weaves,
With rhymes and puns in tangled leaves!
A joyful quill, a vibrant stain,
Nature's humor spills, like happy rain.

Petal-Laden Thoughts Unfurled

In clouds of blooms, the thoughts parade,
A daffodil dons a flashy shade.
With smiles they spread, like butter on toast,
Each bloom a punchline, laugh we boast!

The orchids whisper a witty pun,
'We're late for tea, but oh, such fun!'
In this field of jest, the colors shine,
Each shade a quirk, each stem divine.

Sunflowers strut, so tall and proud,
'Look at me!' they shout, and draw a crowd.
The lilacs chuckle, in purple gleam,
Sharing secrets of their scented dream.

What joy it is in floral glee,
Where laughter blooms and hearts run free!
In every petal's soft embrace,
We find a joke, a sweet, warm place.

Verses from a Flowered Heart

In rows of color, verses sway,
A tulip teases, 'Come dance and play!'
Petals flutter in silly spray,
What a comical blend, hip-hip-hooray!

A garden's laugh is quite the treat,
With daisies giggling at bees' small feet.
They toss yellow confetti, so bright and gay,
Nature's slapstick; who needs a bouquet?

The zinnias boast of their vibrant hues,
'You think you're bright? We've got the views!'
And roses roll their eyes, say 'Oh dear,
In this flowery comedy, it's all clear!'

With each soft rustle, a joke's unfurled,
The blooms unite, hilarity swirled.
In this heart of flowers, joy takes flight,
A bouquet of laughter, pure delight!

The Language of Flora and Feelings

Beneath the sun, wit blooms in rows,
A lily declares, 'I'm dressed to pose!'
The violets whisper, 'Shh, keep it low,'
Each word a giggle, in breezy flow.

The sunflowers turn, with a cheeky grin,
'We're roots and shoots, let the fun begin!'
With leafy laughter and petals adrift,
These nature jesters give the best gift.

A garden's glee in colors so wild,
Where daisies draw maps and bees go wild.
There's no sad face in this lively space,
Just blooms with a joke, each soft embrace.

So let's raise a glass with a sprout so spry,
To the fun in flora, oh my, oh my!
In petals' chatter, we find our tune,
With nature's laughter, we dance by the moon.

Scroll of Floral Whimsy

A tulip told a joke to me,
It giggled in the breeze and glee.
A daisy winked from cheek to cheek,
Said, "My humor's quite unique!"

The roses rolled their eyes with grace,
While violets danced in funny place.
"I'm the punchline!" the lilies sang,
As sunshine hit and meadow rang.

The daisies tossed a punnish grin,
"Look who's petal-ing, join the din!"
A shared joke streamed in colors bright,
Nature's giggles, pure delight!

So here's to blooms with wit so sly,
Each flower blooms, and blooms ask why.
In this silly garden's game,
Funny blooms will never wane!

A Tapestry of Nature's Script

The kitten napped in tangled grass,
While butterflies just soared on past.
A leafy bard began to strum,
Then sang of bees who always hum.

The sunflower stretched, arm like a shroud,
"I'm the tallest one in this crowd!"
The daffodils in gossip spun,
"Let's bloom where there's more sun, just fun!"

In this lyrical field, thoughts arise,
With silly winds and silly skies.
A flower's tale takes a twist or two,
Laughing petals in morning dew!

So gather 'round in nature's fair,
With giggles woven everywhere.
In this bright, floral mystery,
A snicker blooms, wild and free!

Fragrance Etched in Verse

In the meadow where dreams take flight,
Scented verses dance in delight.
A rose remarked on silly days,
"Why do bees wear polka dots? No way!"

The lilacs laughed with fragrant flair,
Emitting giggles in the air.
Bounce back and forth, the blooms conspire,
In nature's script, they never tire.

The daisies dressed in stripes of cheer,
Said, "Well, isn't this just grand, my dear?"
A chorus sang, "Let's not be plain,
Wear colors bright, we'll entertain!"

So scents entangle in a comical scene,
With chuckles blooming bright and keen.
The story's written, surely pure,
In the garden's heart, we all endure!

Blooms Beneath the Writing

Paper chirps with scribbled wit,
As blooms below add to the skit.
"Why did the gremlin cross the lane?"
"His friends were rooting, go insane!"

A meandering breeze shared a pun,
Blowing whispers, oh what fun!
With flowers in riotous rhyme,
Nature's laughter, all in time.

Petals twitched with life anew,
Writing tales of mischief too.
Chortling daisies joined the spree,
As butterflies laughed with glee!

A cascade of laughter spilled like ink,
In nature's plot, oh how we think!
The paper chuckled, grinning wide,
For blooms and ink are quite allied!

A Garden Written in Colors

In a garden where crayons bloom,
Colors frolic, dispelling gloom.
Each shade giggles, slaps a knee,
A rainbow's laughter, wild and free.

With each stroke, the daisies dance,
Making art a splendid chance.
Silly violets wear a smile,
Tickling sunflowers all the while.

The canvas splatters, quite a treat,
As tulips hop on tiny feet.
A paintbrush tickles, colors clash,
Creating chaos—oh, what a splash!

When the sky cries, colors run,
A laughing puddle, oh so fun!
In this garden, joy's the muse,
Where laughter's blooms never lose.

Lines Twined with Floral Essence

Lines twined with blooms, oh what a sight,
Giggles dance in the moonlight.
Witty petals, quips set free,
In this garden, bloom with glee.

Daffodils whisper silly jokes,
As daisies dance with playful folks.
Ink spills laughter from bees' lips,
Wordy blooms take countless trips.

Tulips wear hats, oh what a scene,
While roses tease, looking so keen.
Chasing sunbeams, blossoms race,
Chortles echo in their pace.

In every bud, a punchline waits,
Flowered humor celebrates.
A line of laughter, rogue and bold,
In this garden, joy unfolds.

The Verses of a Secret Garden

In a secret garden, whispers flow,
Cacti giggle, putting on a show.
Amidst the blooms, jokes take flight,
Tickled petals are pure delight.

Witty zinnias craft their tales,
As daisies skate on giddy trails.
Naughty nettles poke and tease,
While sleepy buds dance with ease.

Each leaf a stanza, bright and spry,
In this paradise, laughter's nigh.
Curling vines with punchlines tight,
Crackling giggles under the light.

Oh, what joys behind each leaf,
Petals laughing, beyond belief.
In secret corners, cheer is found,
In verses where the fun abounds.

Sonnet of Blossoms and Ink

Sonnet penned with flowers' ink,
Playful petals dance and wink.
Each stanza bursts with jokes to share,
As blooms spin tales without a care.

Orchids chuckle with a sway,
While tulips prank the bees' ballet.
Vivid lines that twist and twine,
Creating laughter, sweet and fine.

In a verse where colors play,
Daffodils will steal the day.
Nectar drips from tips of leaves,
Jokingly hiding, hearts it cleaves.

In this sonnet, flowers blend,
A tableau rich with joy, my friend.
Through vibrant phrases, smiles will bloom,
As blossoms burst in colorful rooms.

Scribbles Beneath Canopies of Petals

In gardens where the daisies giggle,
The ants hold meetings, all in a wiggle.
Sunflowers bow to the light on their face,
While bees gossip sweetly, keeping up pace.

Beneath the trees, in shades of delight,
Scribbles from squirrels take off in flight.
A cat strikes a pose, with a flowered hat,
While butterflies flutter, all chatting like that.

The wind whispers secrets to blossoms so bright,
While worms write haikus in the dim morning light.
A frog croaks a tune, not quite on the beat,
As laughter erupts from the root of a seat.

So raise your glass, let the petals twirl,
To nature's odd rhythm, let joy unfurl.
For under the canopies, we dance and we play,
In this jumbled, wiggly, fun-filled display.

The Artistry of Nature's Prose

A daffodil drafts a letter to the breeze,
While butterflies practice their wittiest tease.
Bees hum a tune, a melodic applause,
As flowers debate the silliest laws.

A dandelion sighs, 'I'm a wish today!'
While nearby, a rabbit hops, ready to sway.
Forget-me-nots giggle, their laughter profound,
As clouds float above, tracing shapes on the ground.

The ivy creeps in to steal all the scenes,
While roses write sonnets in splendid routines.
A toadstool declares it's the overlord here,
And the tomatoes just blush, feeling quite queer.

So listen closely, nature's words are a laugh,
With every rustle, a gleeful autograph.
In this book of life, let us read and compose,
For artistry blooms in the prose nature chose.

Blooms Bound in Written Whimsy

In a meadow where the imagination flows,
The wildflowers write tales of their highs and lows.
A bumblebee scribbles in yellow on green,
While daisies create scenes that are rarely seen.

A clover discusses with thistles their plight,
As daisies argue who can twirl just right.
Every color knows its own little plot,
Creating a world that's wonderfully hot.

In the hush of the evening, with laughter and cheer,
Lilies pen jokes for the night's sky to hear.
Their petals are pages, turning soft in the breeze,
With laughter lurking 'neath the trees like a tease.

So gather your thoughts where the blossoms stay bound,
In whimsical tales where the fun can be found.
For in this live story, written with glee,
The blooms share their laughter, and we laugh with thee.

A Serenade in the Petal's Shadow

In twilight's embrace, the roses take lead,
With a chorus of giggles, they plant every seed.
Tulips dress up in their best spring attire,
As lilies perform on a stage made of fire.

A squirrel juggles acorns, trying to impress,
While grasshoppers dance in a fancy dress mess.
Beneath the old oak, a skunk writes a rhyme,
About moonlight mischief, all happening in time.

Crickets accompany with their chirpy delight,
As fireflies twinkle, lighting up the night.
The blossoms all sway in a rhythmic display,
As they serenade softly, their worries at bay.

So laugh with the blooms as they celebrate so,
In the shadows where mischief and fun always flow.
For every leaf whispers a secret or two,
In this garden of laughter, I share it with you.

The Tapestry of Flora and Form

In a garden where the daisies talk,
The tulips strut and take a walk,
The roses wear their thorns with pride,
While sunflowers gaze at skies so wide.

Bees buzzing like they know the score,
While butterflies aimlessly adore,
Each bloom a joker in this show,
With petals dancing to and fro.

The violets whisper tales of fun,
In their purple gowns beneath the sun,
While daisies giggle, make a wish,
For a bird to land and steal their dish.

And when the clouds sip on some rain,
The garden laughs, it feels no pain,
Life's a joke when blooms engage,
In this silly, colorful stage.

Verses Painted with Nature's Brush

In colors bright, a painting's made,
With blooms that laugh, their fears allayed,
The daisies chuckle, 'Look who's here!'
While honeybees buzz without a care.

The roses blush with laughter's grace,
As marigolds join the cheerful race,
Even the weeds, in their scruffy way,
Try to join in the lyrical play.

A wind will gust, and petals fly,
Like love notes written to the sky,
They swirl around, a crazy dance,
Each flower hoping for a chance.

So gather 'round, all creatures dear,
Join the chorus, lend an ear,
For nature's laughter fills the air,
In vibrant hues beyond compare.

Chronicles of the Unfolding Blossoms

Once upon a time in sturdy dirt,
A bud dreamed big, oh what a flirt!
With giggles shared among the green,
Each bloom rejoiced, a lively scene.

The lilacs whispered cheeky tales,
As cosmos spun their flowery sails,
And each petal wore its own crown,
In this confetti-colored town.

Daffodils donned sunglasses bright,
Basking in the warmth of light,
While pumpers strummed on blades of grass,
Making melodies that pass.

So here's the plot, a bloom's delight,
In the garden, everything feels right,
Let's toast to laughter, let's sing out loud,
For blossoms chuckle, they're so proud!

The Inked Symphony of Garden Life

In the ink of dusk, blooms come alive,
With shaggy petals that wink and jive,
The garden plays a symphony true,
Of giggles, grins, and morning dew.

Snapdragons snap at the bumblebee,
While daisies shout, 'Come dance with me!'
The pansies prance as if in a race,
With sun-kissed cheeks, oh what a face!

And when the moon begins to rise,
The night blooms whisper sweet goodbyes,
Yet vow to play again at dawn,
As laughter echoes, forever drawn.

So let's ink this tale, oh what a way,
For blossoms bask in playful sway,
In every petal, laughter's trace,
A garden full of joy and grace.

The Garden's Literary Embrace

In the garden of words, I wander and roam,
Where daisies write poems and violets comb.
A sunflower's smile, it brightens the prose,
And weeds tell tall tales, I suppose!

The tomatoes debate, their topics quite ripe,
While onions form sonnets with juicy hype.
A pepper disputes with a bold, fiery flair,
While the lettuce just giggles, without a care!

The roses recite about love in the breeze,
While pansies just chuckle and tease with such ease.
A daffodil's quip, oh, how it does bloom,
Painting the garden with laughter, not gloom!

So join in this dance with the flowers and lore,
In this whimsical place where we all can explore.
They scribble their stories with sunshine and cheer,
In the garden of laughter, come join us right here!

Stanzas Among the Flowerbeds

In a flowerbed corner, the daisies convene,
With petals of sarcasm, quite candid and keen.
A pansy jokes 'bout the bees' busy day,
While roses roll laughter in their own way!

The tulips recite lines so fluffy and fun,
While the marigolds giggle, chasing the sun.
The violets gossip, their secrets in bloom,
Sharing the news of a rabbit's wild zoom!

The lilacs complain of the squirrels' loud chatter,
While wisterias waltz, unbothered by splatter.
Each bloom has a story to share with delight,
In this patch of absurdity, everything's bright!

As the petals sway gently, harmony reigns,
These verses of chuckles, where joy never wanes.
So slip off your shoes, let the laughter cascade,
In the flowerbed stanzas, become unafraid!

Blooms Between the Lines

In the margins of books, blossoms chuckle and play,
With meanings that twist like a wiggly stray.
A fern offers wisdom on pages so crammed,
While roses roll dice, their fortune pre-banned!

Petunias pen poems, their colors on cue,
While sunflowers pencil in jokes just for you.
The lilacs take turns, their tales bloom with flair,
As violets whisper, 'Please, share if you dare!'

The garden's a scribe, in its leafy attire,
With punchlines that sprout, igniting the fire.
Each petal's a letter, a giggle in print,
In this literary space, life's never quite stint!

So flip through the stanzas, let laughter unfold,
This symphony of blooms, with each tale retold.
In the cozy embrace of this leaf-laden floor,
Find joy in the pages, and always seek more!

The Secret Language of Flowers

In the hush of the garden, the blooms start to chat,
With gossip so juicy, it's next-level brat.
A rose asks a lily about fashion and flair,
While daisies keep secrets, lost in the air!

Tulips plot mischief, their colors ablaze,
While peonies' laughter could dazzle and amaze.
The orchids make winks, with a petal-thin grin,
In this secretive club, it's all giggles within!

With every exchange, a tale blooms anew,
A marigold's joke can brighten your view.
The sweet scents of humor intertwine with the breeze,
In this radiant space, where the laughter brings ease!

So lean in a little, let the flowers just speak,
Their giggles and whispers will make your week.
In the secretive garden, where humor exudes,
Join the flowery banter; there's no need for feuds!

Petaled Memories in Written Form

Once a flower wrote a tale,
Upon a napkin, it set sail.
The ink was mixed with honeydew,
And read aloud to quite a few.

But bees came buzzing, oh so sly,
They mistook it for a pie.
They flipped the napkin, lost their way,
And now, they buzz in disarray!

A daffodil claimed to be wise,
Said, "Watch me write, you'll be surprised!"
But tangled roots and floppy stem,
Had it scribble like a drunken gem.

We laugh at flowers, tales they weave,
For beauty's laugh, we can't believe.
Their written words, a comical sight,
In gardens where the sun shines bright.

Nature's Script upon the Leaves

In whispered winds, the leaves do chat,
Accusing bugs of stealing fat.
With every rustle, they share a joke,
About the squirrel who tried to poke.

A lazy vine, with ink-stained hands,
Drew funny faces on the strands.
It giggled as the flowers glanced,
At carrot tops in a weird dance!

The oak's bad puns go far and wide,
With every bark, it swells with pride.
But nearby, a willow rolled its eyes,
"Stop with the jokes, it's time to rise!"

Through every leaf, a story flows,
With laughter bright where laughter grows.
So when you stroll through woods so deep,
Remember jokes the branches keep.

Inked Blossoms through Time's Glass

A daisy penned a sonnet sweet,
But forgot to use its feet.
It spilled the ink, and oh, the mess!
Now every verse is just a test!

Pansies giggled, rolled on by,
"Give us your best, we'll use our eye!"
They scrawled their rhymes on petals bright,
Oh dear, those blooms just took flight!

The tulip claimed it's a poet's muse,
With rhymes so grand, it'll never lose.
But when it tripped on its own lines,
The whispers turned to chuckle signs.

Each blossom writes but none can sing,
Still, charm flows from everything.
So gather 'round and hear the glee,
In blooms that write, oh can't you see?

Pages of Blooming Whispers

On a page was a sneaky bloom,
Whispering jokes in the afternoon.
It told a rose about a bee,
Who mistook a petal for a key!

The marigold laughed till it turned red,
"Did you hear? The tulips fled!"
Writing notes on scents and charms,
Each petal swayed with funny arms.

In gardens held by giggles bright,
The daisies danced into the night.
With every word, the laughter grew,
Ink and flowers held their brew.

So flip the pages, read along,
Nature holds a joyful song.
Every bloom, with heart so sly,
Turns words to chuckles, oh my my!

Verses Woven with Petal Softness

In a garden where words twirl and spin,
The daisies gossip, the tulips grin.
A rhyming bee buzzes, lost in delight,
Jotting down tales till the fall of night.

The roses giggle, wearing a crown,
While violets slouch in their leafy gown.
A daffodil dreams of being a star,
But just ends up planting a joke from afar.

The sunflowers chuckle, with faces aglow,
As bees drop punchlines that surely flow.
Each quip in the air, like fresh spring air,
Makes writing a flora-filled giggle affair.

So pen your thoughts with a petal soft tune,
Let laughter bloom, like flowers in June.
For in this garden where humor thrives,
Each word is a bud that joyfully dives.

Ink and Flora Dance in Harmony

With ink on the page, the flowers revolt,
They swap writers' pens for a wacky jolt.
The lilies leaped, nipping at prose,
While orchids stitched together farce, so it grows.

A dandelion snorts, creating a breeze,
As poems take flight with the greatest of ease.
The daisies choreograph a cute little jig,
While the ferns narrate tales of a giant pig.

In this quirky dance, with roots intertwined,
Stories grow wild, whimsically designed.
A laughter-filled plot takes hold of the sun,
Where humor and flora make writing great fun.

So jot down your thoughts like blossoms of cheer,
For the joy of the garden is ever so near.
Join the ink and the petals in a zesty ballet,
And let your imagination frolic and play!

A Garden of Written Wonders

Amidst a garden bright with silly things,
The flowers are plotting to take off their rings.
A sunflower shimmies, a daffodil sweeps,
As the marigolds plot their giggly leaps.

With each line that blooms, the whimsy expands,
The roses brew mischief with tiny bands.
A poem-shaped cucumber rolls off the shelf,
Praising the author, "You're quite the elf!"

The lilacs all whisper, "What's next on the page?"
"More silliness!" chuckles a well-read sage.
Each verse that emerges from laughter's embrace,
Makes this backyard wonder a funny place.

So gather your thoughts, let your humor unfold,
Within this garden, let stories be bold.
With each little bud, and each chuckle shared,
A tapestry of joy, beautifully aired.

The Blooming Narrative

In a tale where the flowers break into song,
The petals are prancing, they can't help but throng.
A daisy declares it's the queen of the rhyme,
While tulips cite verses that tickle with time.

The garden is filled with puns that are fresh,
The violets insist—"We're a punny mesh!"
A whimsical grape vine twirls through the scene,
Crafting sketches of stories most lightly obscene.

Each flower around spills laughter like dew,
As giggles sprout freely, the humor just grew.
They scribble their dreams in soft morning light,
Imagining capers that take off in flight.

So pen your own story with sport and good cheer,
Let laughter take root, let your worries disappear.
For in this blooming tale of amusing delight,
The garden of words brings a smile so bright.

Whispers of the Blooming Ink

In a garden where words go to play,
The ink spills secrets, come what may.
Flowers giggle in brilliant hue,
Telling tales of what they knew.

A daisy once wore a bowler hat,
Claiming it was quite the chat!
While roses flirt in crimson red,
They gossip about an ill-timed thread.

Sunflowers dance with a snappy beat,
Twirling 'round with two left feet.
Hyacinths joke, 'We're no pretenders!'
As bees buzz 'round with flowery fenders.

So let's write down in flowing ink,
The laughter shared with each bright wink.
For in this garden, humor grows,
Where every petal whirls and glows.

Fragments of Flora and Verse

Once a lilac dreamed of a quilt,
Sewed with lines from a playful wilt.
A tulip claimed it stole the show,
While daisies rolled in the grass below.

In a pot, a cactus grinned wide,
'I'm prickly, but it's quite a ride!'
'You all wear colors, but I stay green,'
Said he, outsmarting the flowered scene.

The violets whisper with gleeful cheer,
'What's the gnome doing hanging near?'
Flowers chuckle, it's quite the spree,
As daisies tease, 'Oh, let him be!'

So gather your scribbles, let's not delay,
This garden's a page with much to say.
In every bloom, a comic line,
Where rhymes are woven and laughter shines.

Echoes of a Garden's Story

In the quiet where fragrances sing,
A flower's tale makes the heart zing.
An orchid quips in a snobby tone,
'Noticing your looks, could I loan you a bone?'

The violets team up with lazy bees,
Hovering softly in fragrant breeze.
'We'll steal the show,' they say with glee,
While tulips pout in jealousy.

Down by the pond, a lily did grin,
'My reflection's much better than him!'
With ripples that dance, their laughter rings,
As frogs join in for the joy it brings.

So journal your thoughts in colorful ink,
Join this garden, and let us wink.
For every blossom tells a tale,
Of humor, blooms, and windswept gales.

The Inked Blossoms of Memory

Once I found a flower with a hat,
Worn crookedly, imagine that!
It told me stories of ink and dreams,
In a world where nothing's as it seems.

The daisies wrestled with breezy jest,
While sunflowers claimed they were the best.
'You'd be surprised,' laughed a sneaky weed,
'How much fun our wild roots can breed.'

A group of pansies began to dance,
Flaunting their colors, in a trance.
As bumblebees buzzed truths half a mile,
The garden echoed with laughter and style.

So let's pencil in these joyful days,
Where flowers bloom in whimsical ways.
For every memory, twinkling bright,
Is inked in colors that bring delight.

Secrets Held in Fragile Leaves

Whispers of giggles, oh what a tale,
Leaves leap with secrets, like mice in a pail.
Fluttering softly, they tumble and glide,
Each one a giggle, a little joyride.

Crisp edges rustle, with laughter they play,
Falling like feathers, in a breezy ballet.
Tickles from breezes, they shimmy and sway,
Unlocking the mischief held deep in their stay.

In the thick of the garden, sly smiles take flight,
Where gossiping blossoms share stories at night.
The leaves hold their laughter, a comedic parade,
Secrets in colors, in shade and in jade.

So next time you wander, look down at the ground,
You might find a giggle, or a chuckle profound.
For nature's a joker, on stages of green,
In secrets of leaves, more than we've seen.

Dances of Color on White Canvas

On a canvas so bright, colors twist and tangle,
Dancing with joy, oh what a wrangle!
Crimson with laughter, the yellows go wild,
In the rhythm of brushstrokes, every hue's a child.

Swirls of confetti spread joy without care,
As blues do a jig like they just won a fair.
Splashes of orange throw their hands in the air,
While violets giggle, their laughter to share.

Strokes frolic freely, with chortles and grins,
An orchestra painted, where everybody spins.
The white canvas chuckles, a scene so absurd,
Where colors are dancing, and high fives are heard!

When hues start to laugh, and the brush takes a leap,
Art's not just serious; it also can peep.
The waltz of the colors, it never grows old,
On canvases blank, funny stories unfold.

Stanzas in the Garden of Dreams

In a garden of dreams where the wild laughter grows,
Each flower is chatting, oh what a show!
Daisies are gossiping, tulips in glee,
While roses are snorting at jokes by the tree.

Dandelions dance, with a bounce and a spin,
Sharing their secrets, where silliness begins.
Sunflowers chuckle, their heads high and bright,
As the violets snicker at the butterflies' flight.

In this playful patch, the shadows just romp,
With a skip and a hop, they all do the stomp.
Every petal's a punchline, clever and quick,
Where laughter's the language, and joy is the trick.

So wander these stanzas, with whimsy and cheer,
In the garden of dreams, where humor is near.
No solemnity here, just giggles and beams,
In this vibrant oasis, where all is as it seems.

Fragrance of Words in Full Bloom

Words flutter like blossoms, sprouting with wit,
Blooming with laughter, never to quit.
The scents of their joy fill the air all around,
Where each phrase is a tickle, and giggles abound.

Whimsical whispers float gently in air,
Jokes blossom out loud, filling hearts without care.
Phrases like petals, in colorful flight,
Bringing cheer to the day, turning dark into light.

With a whiff of the silly, and a breeze from the fun,
The garden of words is for everyone!
So stretch out your senses, let laughter arise,
In the fragrance of language, see joy in disguise.

So pluck all the phrases, sweet and absurd,
In this fragrant fiesta, let's spread every word.
For smiles are the blossoms, and laughter's the bloom,
In the garden of language, we find our own room.

www.ingramcontent.com/pod-product-compliance
Lightning Source LLC
Chambersburg PA
CBHW071835160426
43209CB00003B/309